THE EUGÉNIE ROCHEROLLE SERIES

Intermediate Piano Solo

Swingin' the Blues

6 Original Solos by Eugénie Rocherolle

T0081962

Cover Photo © Peter Amft

ISBN-13: 978-1-4234-3206-7
ISBN-10: 1-4234-3206-1

HAL•LEONARD®
CORPORATION

7777 W. BLUEMOUND RD. P.O. BOX 13819 MILWAUKEE, WI 53213

In Australia Contact:
Hal Leonard Australia Pty. Ltd.
4 Lentara Court
Cheltenham, Victoria, 3192 Australia
Email: ausadmin@halleonard.com

Visit Hal Leonard Online at
www.halleonard.com

TWO-WAY BLUES

By EUGÉNIE ROCHEROLLE

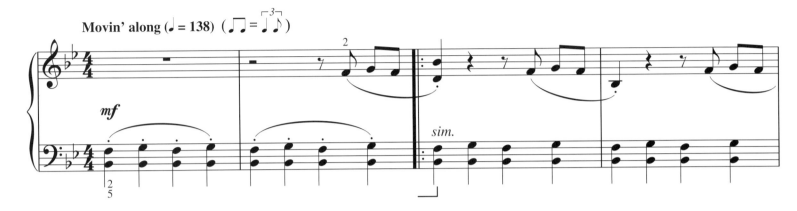

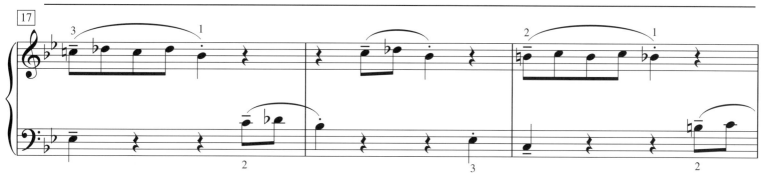

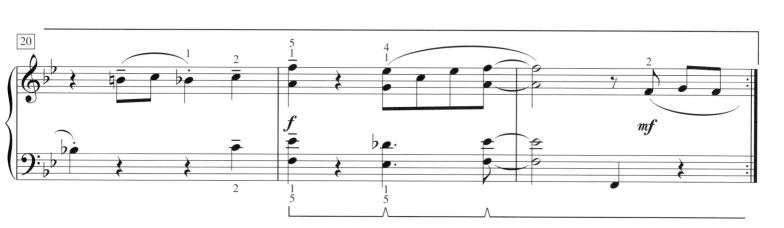

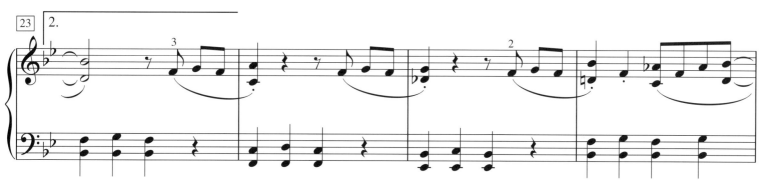

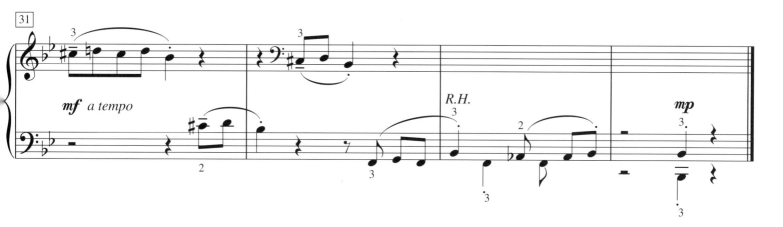

HOMETOWN BLUES

By EUGÉNIE ROCHEROLLE

Moderately (♩ = 108)

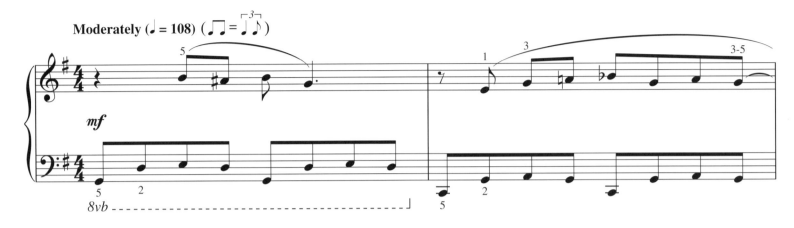

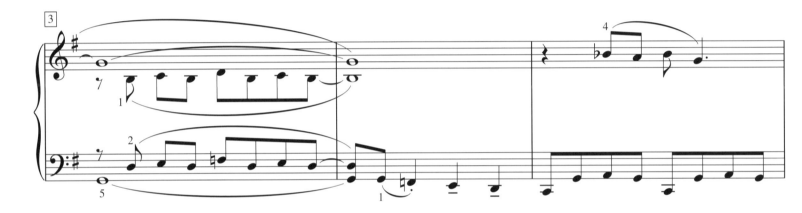

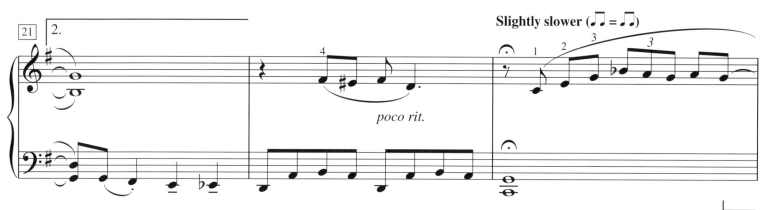

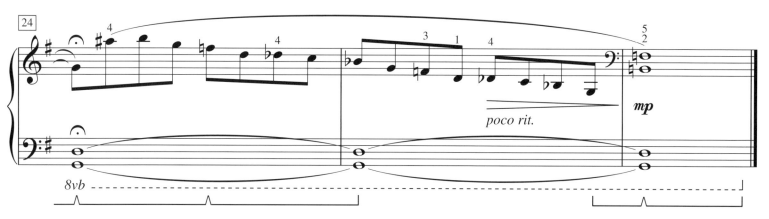

EASY WALKIN' BLUES

By EUGÉNIE ROCHEROLLE

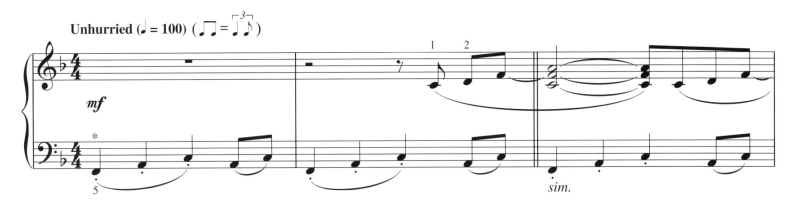

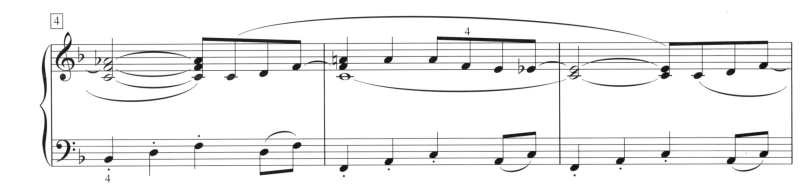

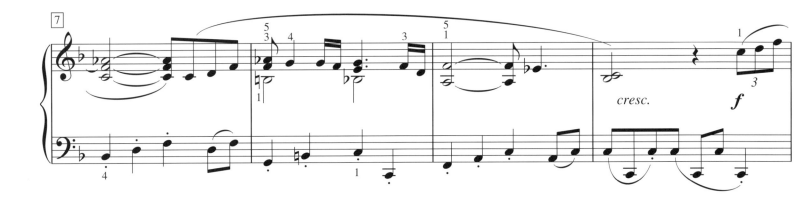

* all staccatos are *mezzo staccato*

7

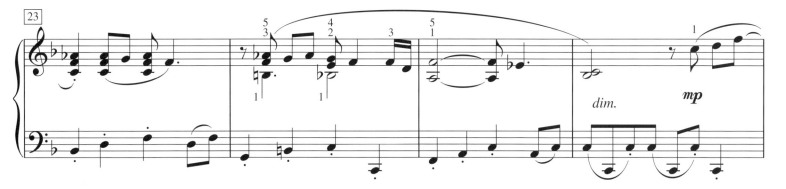

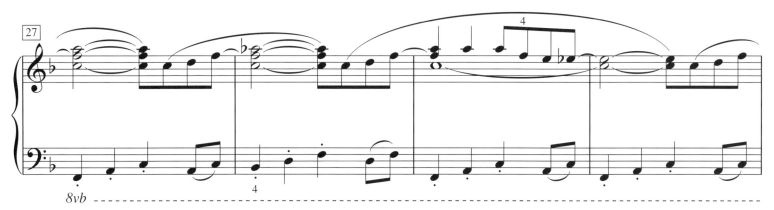

BACK STREET BLUES

By EUGÉNIE ROCHEROLLE

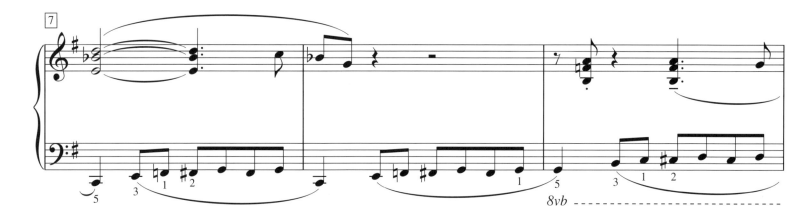

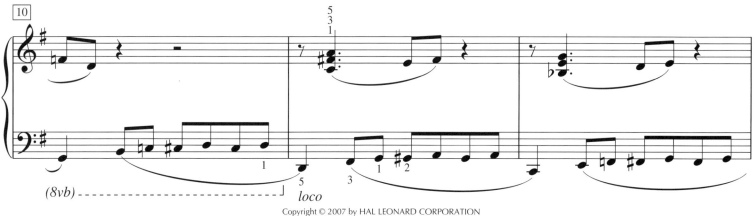

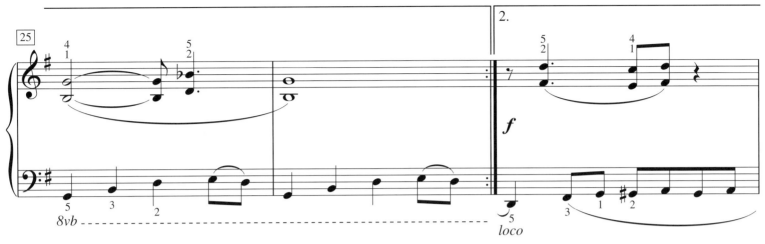

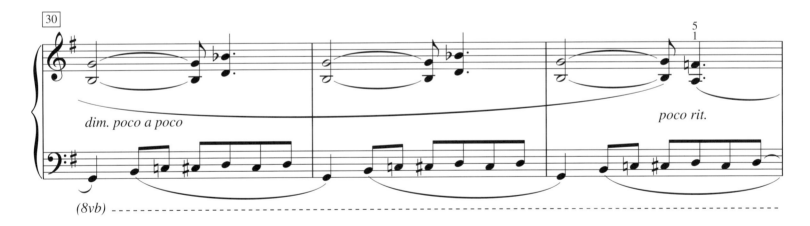

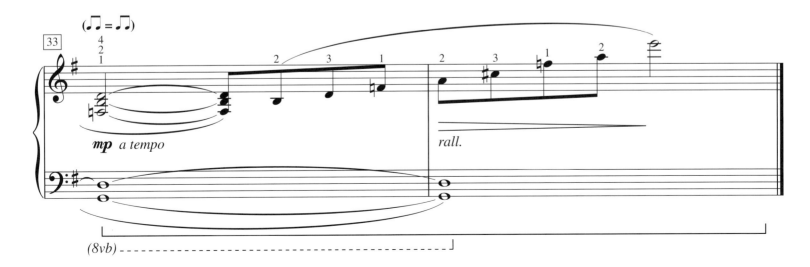

BIG SHOT BLUES

By EUGÉNIE ROCHEROLLE

Steady beat (♩ = 104)

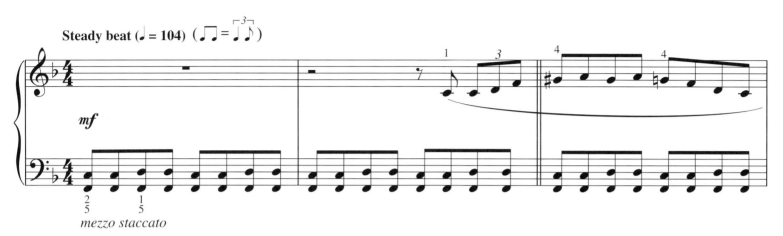

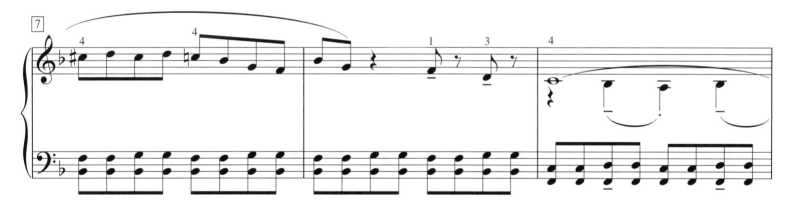

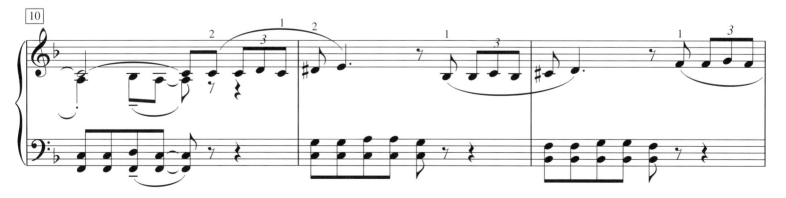

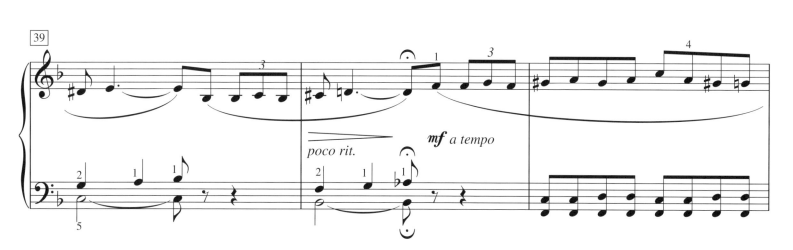

LATE NIGHT BLUES

By EUGÉNIE ROCHEROLLE

With a slow swing (♩ = 84)

simile

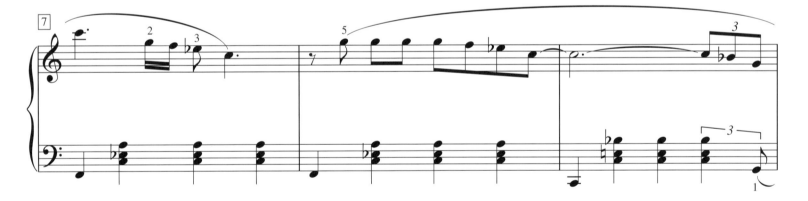

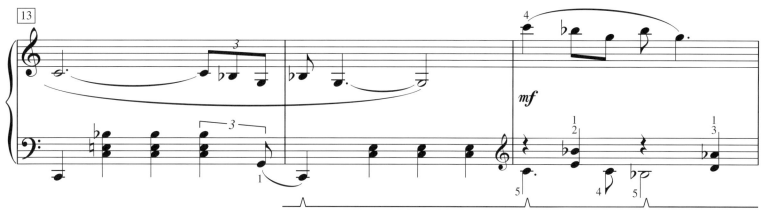

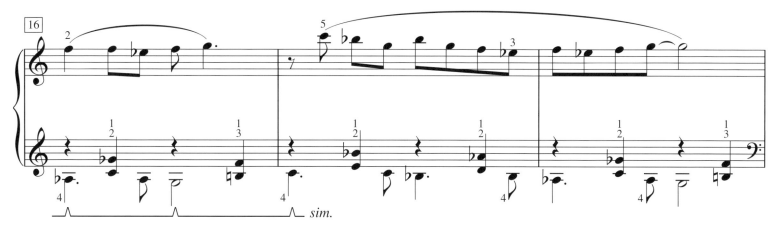

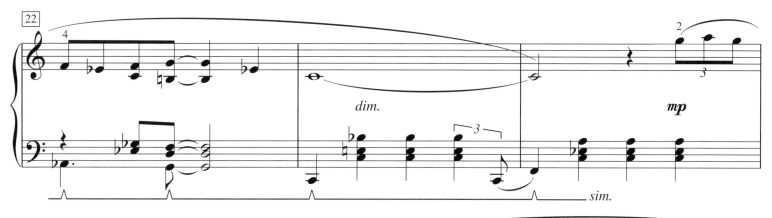

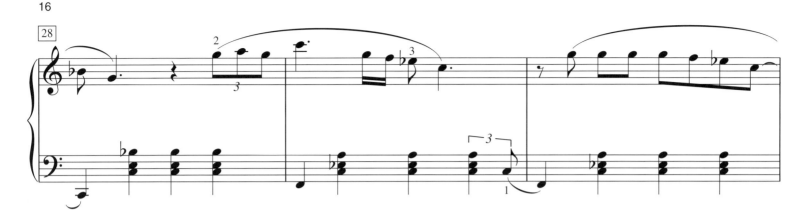

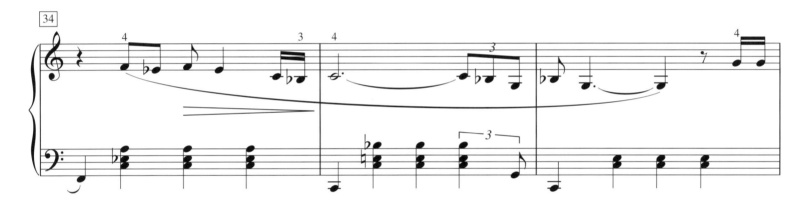

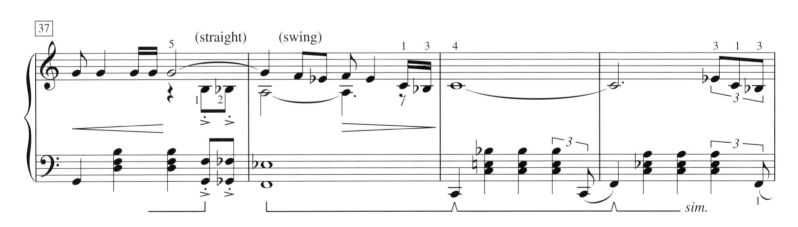